Noisy Bug

Sing-Along

By John Himmelman

DAWN PUBLICATIONS

For Michael DiGiorgio, a fellow fan of noisy bugs — JH

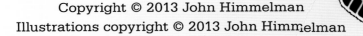

Library of Congress Cataloging-in-Publication Data
Himmelman, John.
  Noisy bug sing-along / by John Himmelman. -- 1st ed.
    p. cm.
  Audience: 3-8
  Summary: "Listen closely to the sounds of insects. Together they make a
concert! Learn about how they do it"-- Provided by publisher.
  ISBN 978-1-58469-191-4 (hardback) -- ISBN 978-1-58469-192-1 (pbk.) 1.
Insect sounds--Juvenile literature. I. Title.
  QL496.5.H56 2013
  595.715--dc23

                         2012024253

Book design and computer production by Patty Arnold, Menagerie Design & Publishing
Manufactured by Regent Publishing Services, Hong Kong
Printed January, 2013, in ShenZhen, Guangdong, China

10 9 8 7 6 5 4 3 2 1
First Edition

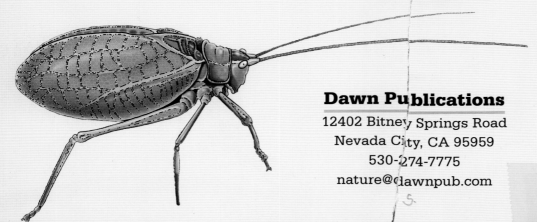

Dawn Publications
12402 Bitney Springs Road
Nevada City, CA 95959
530-274-7775
nature@dawnpub.com

Insects sing both day and night.
Some sing loudly.
Some sing softly.
Sing along with them.

Field Crickets sing from beneath leaves.

CHIRP

Tree Crickets ring like a teleph

REEEEEEEEEEE

REEEEEEEEEE

REEE

Mole Crickets call from a tunnel in the ground.

dirt - dirt - dirt
dirt - dirt - dirt

A Click Beetle clicks as it flips through the air!

CLICK

The Tiger Moth makes very high squeaks when a bat comes too close.

SQUEAKA

A **Dog-Day Cicada** buzzes LOUDLY high in a tree.

ZZZZ

A **Bumble Bee** buzzes softly inside a flower.

Z Z Z Z Z Z Z Z

A Mosquito hums in your ear.

m m m m m m m m m

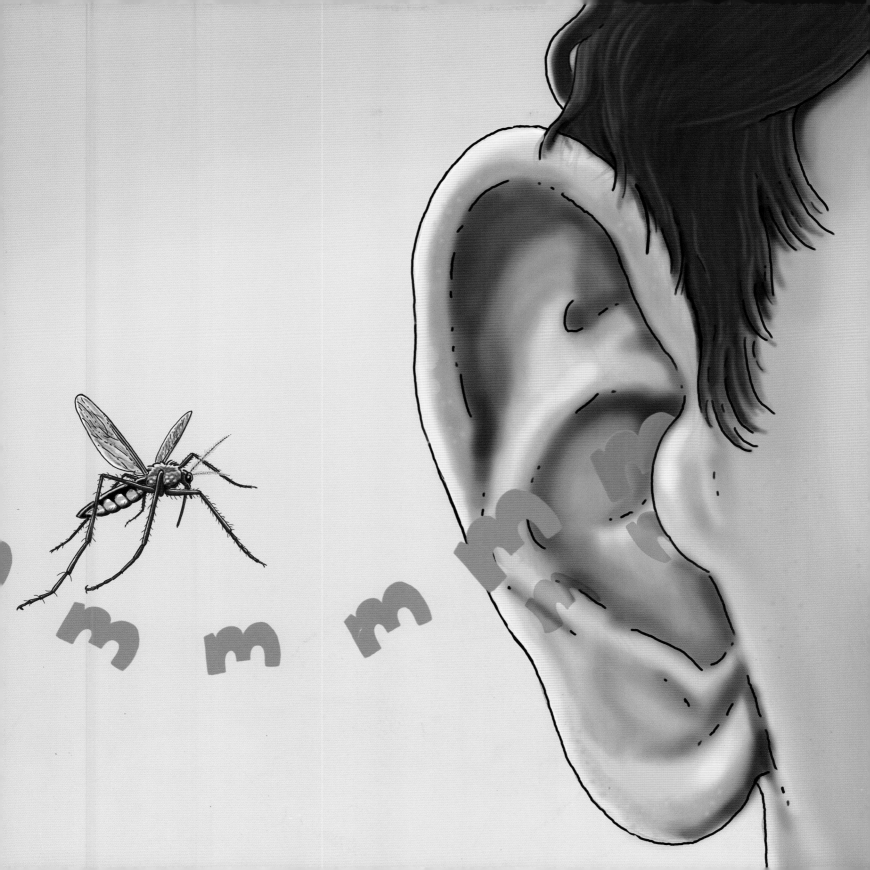

A **Butterfly** flutters by in complete silence.

True Katydids call from the very tops of trees.

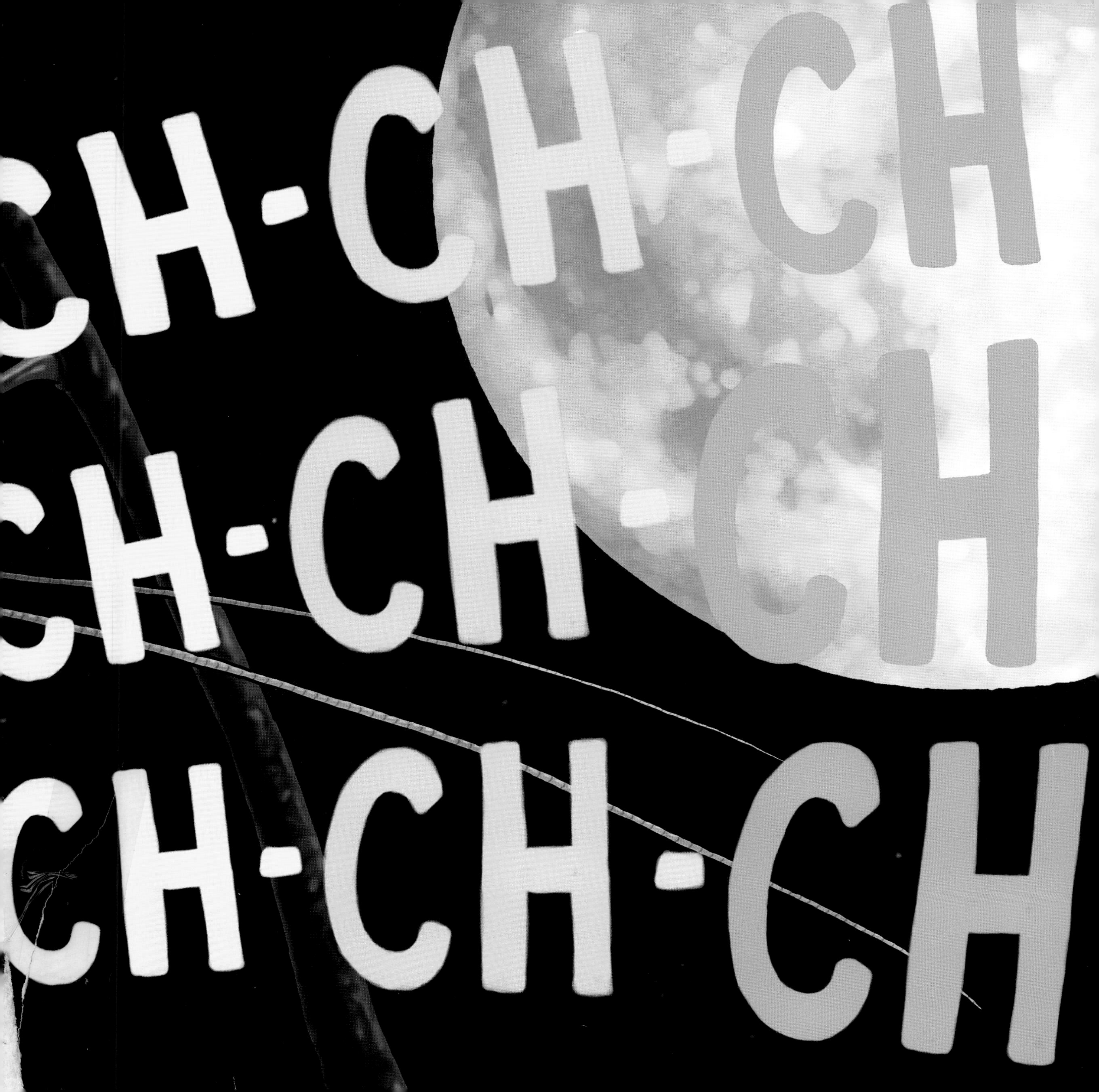
CH-CH-CH
CH-CH-CH
CH-CH-CH

This Bush Katydid sings from a blueberry bush.

tick·tick·tick

zeezeezeezee

A Grasshopper snaps its wings as it floats in the air.

keraaaack

keraaaaack

keraaaack

Together, the insects create a concert of sound.

CHIRP CHIRP CHIRP

SQUEAKA-

m m m m m m m m m m m m m m m m m

RE

ZZZZZZZZZ   silence

RE

CH-CH-CH

Keraaaack   CLICK

CH-CH-CH

CH-CH-CH

tick-tick-tick   Kera

zeezeezeezee

Z Z Z Z Z

dirt-dirt-dirt

tick-tick-

zeezee

SQUEAKA~SQUEAKA

EEEEEEE...

EEEEEEE...

REEEEEEEE...

aacK

ZZZZZZZZZZ

Keraaaack

ZZZZZZZZZZZ

ck

zee

Field Crickets

Tree Crickets

Mole Crickets

Click Beetle

Tiger Moth

Dog Day Cicada

Bumble Bee

Mosquito

Butterfly

True Katydid

Bush Katydid

Grasshopper

Listening to the Noisy Bugs

Sound Waves—and What They REALLY Sound Like
When the bugs move a part of the body to make a sound, they are actually creating a little bit of air pressure that travels through the air as a vibration. This is called a "sound wave." When the bug sounds are recorded, they can be made into sound wave graphs, as shown on the previous page. The height of the line from the middle represents how loud the sound is.

To hear what they *really* sound like, go to www.dawnpub.com/our-books/noisy-bug-sing-along and click on the audio files.

Do it Yourself! Can you imitate the sounds of bugs? They are hard to imitate with your voice, because usually the bugs make the sounds *mechanically* such as by rubbing their forewings together, like the crickets, or by tightening and loosening muscles in their drum-like abdomen, like the cicada. Can you find a way to make similar sounds? You might make an entirely new "insect" sound! Want more? For more insect, bird, frog, and mammal sounds, go to www.musicofnature.org.

Do You Remember? Do you remember which insect makes what sound? Have someone make the sounds, and see if you can remember the insect. Or, have someone name the insect and see if you can remember the sound each one makes. How good are you at recognizing the voices of your friends and classmates?

Bat Ears When compared to many mammals, humans have small ears. But if you cup your hands behind your ears you make them larger and better able to pick up sounds. Try this: go out on a summer night when there is a lot of insect sound. Cup your hands behind your ears to pick out the individual callers. If you tip your head up, you can hear the insects in the trees. Slowly tip your head so you are looking at the horizon and listen for the insects in the shrubs. Tip your head down to the ground to hear the crickets calling from the ground. Then, pull away your hands for an explosion of sound all around!

Travel Without Moving Find a spot in your yard, schoolyard, or a park. Sit, close your eyes, and listen intently. Start by listening to your own breathing. Then "reach out" with your ears to hear every sound close to you. Who, or what, is making those sounds? Extend your listening to as far as you can hear. Imagine the place where those sounds are coming from. While in that one spot, your mind can "ride" those sounds to travel great distances.

Safety in Numbers True Katydids, like the one in this book, will often call together to create a chorus. This can make it difficult for bats to pick out an individual to eat. Here's a game to demonstrate how this works. One blindfolded child (the bat) stands in the middle of a circle of children (the katydids). One katydid claps his or her hands. The bat has to locate this calling katydid by sound, and can usually do so easily! Now, the bat returns to the center. Then ALL the katydids clap together in a pattern. Can the bat find the original katydid? Good luck!

About the Noisy Bugs

Fall Field Crickets *chirp* from beneath logs, rocks and dead leaves. Males begin to chirp in the afternoon and continue through the night. This is how they call females. The call also keeps away other male crickets.

Narrow-winged Tree Crickets have a steady series of long *rings* or trills, each lasting up to 10 seconds. Only the males call. Crickets produce these sounds by rubbing their forewings against each other. They will often chew a hole in the leaf and pop their head through while calling.

Mole Crickets spend most of their lives making tunnels in the dirt. When the male wants to call females, he goes to the edge of his tunnel and rubs his wings together to make the *dirt* sound. The females fly from their burrows to find the singers.

Click Beetles escape danger by flipping in the air. The *click* sound comes from one part of its lower body rubbing quickly against another part. They also click to pop into the air if they find themselves on their back.

Many **Tiger Moths** utter a very high-pitched "*squeaka*" when a bat approaches. The sound is so high-pitched that it's *ultrasonic*, too high for humans to hear. But the bats hear it. Because many tiger moths are poisonous, when they squeak they are saying to the bats, "Don't try to eat me because I'm poisonous."

Dog-Day Cicadas loudly *ZZZZ* by tightening and loosening muscles in their abdomen. The abdomen is hollow, like a drum. This makes the call even louder. While they may look and sound scary, cicadas do not bite or sting.

Bumble Bees vibrate their wings so rapidly that it makes a soft *zzzz*. They use their wing vibrations to shake pollen (their food) from flowers onto their body.

Mosquitoes *humm*, but not because they are singing. Like the buzz of a Bumble Bee, the hum of a mosquito comes from the motion of their wings. Only female mosquitoes drink blood. They are attracted to body heat and the breath of mammals. Male mosquitoes feed on nectar.

Butterflies, like this Clouded Sulphur, are completely silent. They have good eyesight, and don't need sound to find one another. They drink nectar from flowers that are out in the open. Perhaps being silent makes it more difficult for hungry birds to find them.

True Katydids spend most of their lives in the tops of trees, so they are more often heard than seen. They are the loudest katydids in North America. Like most katydids and crickets, their sound is made by rubbing their two outer wings together.

Northern Bush Katydid males sing their *tick-tick-tick- zeezeezeezee* sound to attract females and to scare off other males. They blend with the leaves they live on, but at night they are often attracted to electric lights!

Band-winged Grasshoppers have brightly colored hind wings which can be seen only when they are in flight. At other times, the forewings cover up the hind wings. The males' wings make a *keraaaak* sound when they flutter in the air to attract females.

WHEN JOHN HIMMELMAN WAS EIGHT YEARS OLD, he started his first "Bug Club" in a friend's garage, and he's been playing with insects ever since. Even now, on summer nights John is often in his wooded yard in Killingworth, Connecticut, flashlight in hand, searching for little creatures. Some of his most exciting discoveries are found just a few feet from his house! John co-founded the Connecticut Butterfly Association, is past president of the New Haven Bird Club, and both gives nature programs and makes school visits. He is an author and illustrator of over 75 books for children. John's enthusiasm extends to his family—his wife is an art teacher, his son is an artist, and his daughter is an actress. www.johnhimmelman.com

A FEW OTHER NATURE AWARENESS BOOKS FROM DAWN PUBLICATIONS

In the Trees, Honey Bees — Remarkable inside-the-hive views of bees offer insights into the lives of these important insects.

Under One Rock — A whole community of creatures lives under rocks. No child will be able to resist taking a peek after reading this.

On One Flower — A goldenrod flower is a "minibeast park," have you noticed? Take a closer look . . .

Over in the Ocean: In a Coral Reef is a delightful, energetic counting and singing introduction to ocean animals, part of a best-selling series that also includes *Over in the Jungle*, *Over in the Arctic*, *Over in the Forest* and *Over in Australia*. **This book is now also available as an app — an animated, interactive game!**

Molly's Organic Farm — Wind blows the gate open, and Molly, a homeless cat, scampers through — and discovers the magical interplay of nature on an organic farm. She also finds friendly farmers, and a home.

The BLUES Go Birding — This series of three books is a young person's primer to birds and birdwatching, all entertainingly told as an imaginative travelogue.

Eliza and the Dragonfly — Almost despite herself, Eliza becomes entranced by an "awful" dragonfly nymph—and before long, both of them are transformed. "Magnificent!"

Dawn Publications is dedicated to inspiring in children a deeper understanding and appreciation for all life on Earth. You can browse through our titles, download resources for teachers, and order at www.dawnpub.com or call 800-545-7475.